Autographs

J IS FOR JUDY

Classic Hollywood's
Leading Ladies
from
A to Z

Written by
John Robert Allman

Illustrated by
Peter Emmerich

Doubleday Books
for Young Readers

A is for Audrey, a sudden sensation
when she played a princess in Rome on vacation.

Audrey Hepburn as Princess Ann,
Roman Holiday, 1953

B is for Bette and Barbara, who blazed

Bette Davis as Margo Channing, *All About Eve*, 1950

In radiant roles that amused and amazed.

Barbara Stanwyck as Jean Harrington, *The Lady Eve*, 1941

C's for Joan Crawford, who, like Mildred Pierce,
was driven and dauntless and feisty and fierce.

Joan Crawford as Mildred Pierce, *Mildred Pierce*, 1945

It's also for Carmen, that brilliant Brazilian,
and Carole and Claudette, who were one in a million.

Carmen Miranda as Dorita, *The Gang's All Here*, 1943;
Carole Lombard as Irene Bullock, *My Man Godfrey*, 1936;
Claudette Colbert as Ellie Andrews, *It Happened One Night*, 1934

D is for Debbie and Donna and Doris,

QUIET
PLEASE

THIS
SIDE
UP

Debbie Reynolds as Kathy Selden, *Singin' in the Rain*, 1952; Donna Reed as Mary Hatch, *It's a Wonderful Life*, 1946; Doris Day as Jan Morrow, *Pillow Talk*, 1959

the dynamite Dorothy, and dazzling Dolores.

FRAGILE

Dorothy Dandridge as Carmen Jones, *Carmen Jones*, 1954;
Dolores del Río as Belinha de Rezende, *Flying Down to Rio*, 1933

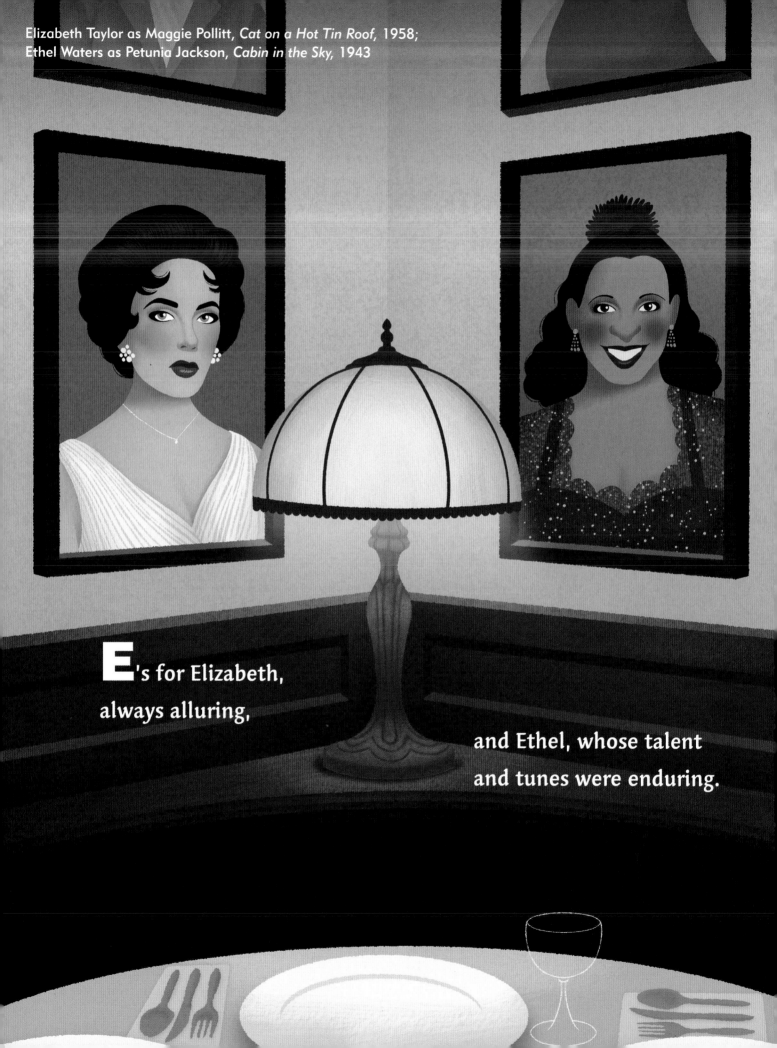

Elizabeth Taylor as Maggie Pollitt, *Cat on a Hot Tin Roof*, 1958;
Ethel Waters as Petunia Jackson, *Cabin in the Sky*, 1943

E's for Elizabeth,
always alluring,

and Ethel, whose talent
and tunes were enduring.

Esther made movies
uniquely aquatic,
a swimmer-turned-star
whose routines were hypnotic.

Esther Williams as Annette Kellerman,

Joan Fontaine as Mrs. de Winter, *Rebecca*, 1940

Kim Novak as Judy Barton, *Vertigo*, 1958

F's Joan Fontaine and her friends who were frightened

Eva Marie Saint as Eve Kendall, *North by Northwest*, 1959

Tippi Hedren as Melanie Daniels, *The Birds*, 1963

in films that were hair-raising, haunting, and heightened.

G is for Ginger, who floated with flair
in the arms of the agile, athletic Astaire.

Ginger Rogers as Dale Tremont (with Fred Astaire as Jerry Travers), *Top Hat*, 1935

Gloria Swanson gave gumption and grit
to a desperate diva who hoped for a hit.

Gloria Swanson as Norma Desmond,
Sunset Boulevard, 1950

H is for Hattie, whose Hollywood highs include taking home the Academy's prize.

Hattie McDaniel at the 12th Academy Awards, 1940

Ingrid, an icon whose skill was immense,
made Ilsa intriguing, ideal, and intense.

Ingrid Bergman as Ilsa Lund, *Casablanca*, 1942

J's Julie and Judy, who couldn't do wrong

Julie Andrews as Maria, *The Sound of Music*, 1965

in the Alps or in Oz when they burst into song.

Judy Garland as Dorothy Gale, *The Wizard of Oz*, 1939

K's Katharine Hepburn, who brimmed with bravado,

Katharine Hepburn as Susan Vance, *Bringing Up Baby*, 1938

and also the breathtaking Katy Jurado.

Katy Jurado as Helen Ramírez, *High Noon*, 1952

Lena and Lupe and Lauren were stars

Lena Horne as Selina Rogers, *Stormy Weather*, 1943

in musicals, comedies, and in film noirs.

Lupe Vélez as Carmelita Fuentes, *The Girl from Mexico*, 1939;
Lauren Bacall as Marie "Slim" Browning, *To Have and Have Not*, 1944

M's for Marlene
and Marilyn, too,

Marlene Dietrich as Mademoiselle Amy Jolly, Morocco, 1930

as two savvy singers
who sparkled on cue.

Marilyn Monroe as Lorelei Lee, *Gentlemen Prefer Blondes*, 1953

N is for Natalie, Norma, and Nancy,
in flicks that were daring, dramatic, and dancy.

Natalie Wood as Judy, *Rebel Without a Cause*, 1955 (top left); Norma Shearer as Mrs. Stephen Haines
(Mary), *The Women*, 1939 (top right); Nancy Kwan as Linda Low, *Flower Drum Song*, 1961 (bottom)

O's for Olivia (Joan Fontaine's sister).
As shy Catherine Sloper, it's hard to resist her.

Olivia de Havilland as Catherine Sloper, *The Heiress*, 1949

P's Princess Grace, who made pictures perfection with co-stars like Cary and Hitchcock's direction.

Grace Kelly as Frances Stevens, *To Catch a Thief*, 1955

Q's Queen Christina, presented with passion in Garbo's flamboyant, formidable fashion.

Greta Garbo as Christina, Queen Christina, 1933

R is for Rosalind, Ruby, and Rita,

Rosalind Russell as Hildy Johnson, *His Girl Friday*, 1940;
Ruby Dee as Ruth Younger, *A Raisin in the Sun*, 1961

who triumphed as Hildy and Ruth and Anita.

Rita Moreno as Anita, *West Side Story*, 1961

S is Sophia,
whose famed hands and feet
are imprinted forever
in Grauman's concrete.

Sophia Loren at Grauman's Chinese Theatre, 1962

T's Shirley Temple, the mini-but-mighty,
whose curls and charisma made magic in *Heidi*.

Shirley Temple as Heidi, *Heidi*, 1937

The moving Miyoshi Umeki is **U**.
The Oscars rewarded her stateside debut.

Miyoshi Umeki at the 30th Academy Awards, 1958

V is the versatile Vivien Leigh,
whose breakable Blanche was as brave as could be.

Vivien Leigh as Blanche DuBois, *A Streetcar Named Desire*, 1951

W's wonderful Anna May Wong.
In trailblazing turns, she was stunning and strong.

Anna May Wong as Lan Ying Lin, *Daughter of Shanghai*, 1937

Behind every actress who shines on the screen
is a critical crew of creatives unseen.

MARY PICKFORD

Screenwriter Anita Loos

Director Dorothy Arzner

Actress-producer Mary Pickford

These e**X**perts who edit, craft costumes, or write
made exceptional films that enthrall and excite.

Costume designer Edith Head

Editor Barbara McLean

Choreographer Onna White

Y s for Ms. Young, who was graceful and great
in a holiday hit when she learned how to skate.

Loretta Young as Julia Brougham (with Cary Grant as Dudley), *The Bishop's Wife*, 1947

Z is the glamorous Zsa Zsa Gabor.
With spangles (and spouses), she knew more was more.

Zsa Zsa Gabor as Jane Avril, *Moulin Rouge*, 1952

These ladies are legends, so we recommend:
once you've finished this book, see their movies. . . .

End

JULIE ANDREWS began performing as a child on stage in Britain after World War II and achieved stardom as Eliza Doolittle in Broadway's *My Fair Lady* (1956). She made her film debut in the title role in *Mary Poppins* (1964), winning an Academy Award. The following year, Andrews played yet another iconic screen heroine, Maria in *The Sound of Music* (1965).

DOROTHY ARZNER was Hollywood's only steadily working female director from 1927 until her retirement in 1943. She directed twenty silent and sound films and was instrumental in launching the careers of acclaimed actresses including Katharine Hepburn and Rosalind Russell.

LAUREN BACALL made her film debut at twenty opposite her future husband and frequent co-star, Humphrey Bogart, in *To Have and Have Not* (1944). She worked steadily on screen and stage into her eighties and received an Academy Honorary Award for "her central place in the Golden Age of motion pictures" in 2009.

INGRID BERGMAN astounded audiences of American and European film, television, and theater in dramatic roles. While best remembered as Ilsa in 1942's *Casablanca,* she won her three Academy Awards for *Gaslight* (1944), *Anastasia* (1956), and *Murder on the Orient Express* (1974). She was the mother of actress Isabella Rossellini.

CLAUDETTE COLBERT stopped traffic as Ellie Andrews in 1934's *It Happened One Night,* for which she won an Academy Award. Her tremendous talent earned her two additional Oscar nominations, for *Private Worlds* (1935) and *Since You Went Away* (1944).

JOAN CRAWFORD was a resplendent and resilient star, whose career variously flourished and floundered from the 1920s through the early '70s. Her long résumé is filled with fiercely strong female characters in films such as *The Women* (1939); *Mildred Pierce* (1945), for which she won an Academy Award; and *What Ever Happened to Baby Jane?* (1962).

DOROTHY DANDRIDGE broke racial barriers playing the title role in 1954's *Carmen Jones,* for which she became the first African American to be nominated for an Academy Award for Best Actress and the first African American woman to be featured on the cover of *Life* magazine. She also starred as Bess in the 1959 film adaptation of *Porgy and Bess.*

BETTE DAVIS was a prolific performer whose distinctive dramatics earned her ten Oscar nominations, with two wins: for *Dangerous* (1935) and *Jezebel* (1938). In a career that continued into the 1980s, other triumphant turns included *Now, Voyager* (1942), *All About Eve* (1950), and *What Ever Happened to Baby Jane?* (1962).

DORIS DAY delighted in musicals, comedies, and dramas in the 1950s and '60s, including *Love Me or Leave Me* (1955), *The Man Who Knew Too Much* (1956), and *Pillow Talk* (1959), for which she was nominated for an Academy Award. She later starred in her own sitcom and dedicated herself to animal welfare activism.

RUBY DEE was an Emmy and Grammy Award–winning actress, writer, and activist who originated the role of Ruth Younger in *A Raisin in the Sun* on stage (1959) and screen (1961). Late in her career, she was nominated for an Oscar for *American Gangster* (2007).

OLIVIA DE HAVILLAND was nominated for five Oscars for her work in the 1930s and '40s, winning for *To Each His Own* (1946) and *The Heiress* (1949). She also appeared in *The Adventures of Robin Hood* (1938), *Gone with the Wind* (1939), and *Light in the Piazza* (1962). She was the elder sister of actress Joan Fontaine.

DOLORES DEL RÍO was a Mexican actress, celebrated as Hollywood's first Latin American crossover star. In addition to notable appearances in American silent and sound films in the 1920s and '30s, including *Flying Down to Rio* (1933), in which she starred with Ginger Rogers and Fred Astaire, she was an icon of classic Mexican cinema in the 1940s and '50s.

MARLENE DIETRICH bewitched Berlin on stage and screen before hopping to Hollywood, where she was immortalized in films from *Morocco* (1930), for which she was nominated for an Academy Award, to *Destry Rides Again* (1939) and *Witness for the Prosecution* (1957).

JOAN FONTAINE and Olivia de Havilland are the only sisters to have each won Oscars: Joan was nominated for *Rebecca* (1940) and *The Constant Nymph* (1943) and won for *Suspicion* in 1941, beating Olivia, who was nominated that year for *Hold Back the Dawn*. Fontaine is also the only performer to have won an Academy Award for a film directed by Alfred Hitchcock.

ZSA ZSA GABOR's best film role was the crooning cancan dancer Jane Avril in *Moulin Rouge* (1952). She is remembered as being uniquely herself, with a darling disposition, scintillating style, scene-stealing scandals, and many, many marriages. Her sister Eva Gabor was also an actress.

GRETA GARBO gave powerhouse performances in silent and sound films of the 1920s and '30s—including *Anna Christie* (1930), *Camille* (1936), and *Ninotchka* (1939), all of which earned her Oscar nominations—before retiring at thirty-six in 1941. A private person who avoided publicity, she received an Academy Honorary Award in 1955 "for her unforgettable screen performances" but did not attend the ceremony.

JUDY GARLAND introduced "Over the Rainbow" as Dorothy in 1939's *The Wizard of Oz*, for which she won an Academy Juvenile Award. She starred in twenty-seven mostly musical feature films for MGM from 1937 to 1950, and she was Oscar-nominated for *A Star Is Born* (1954) and *Judgment at Nuremberg* (1961). Garland was the first woman to win the Grammy for Album of the Year, for 1961's *Judy at Carnegie Hall*, and was the mother of stage and screen legend Liza Minnelli.

EDITH HEAD is considered one of the most influential costume designers in Hollywood history. Over the course of her career, she was nominated for thirty-five Oscars and won eight, for films including *The Heiress* (1949), *All About Eve* (1950), *Roman Holiday* (1953), *Sabrina* (1954), and *The Sting* (1973), making her the Academy's all-time most-awarded woman.

TIPPI HEDREN thrilled film fans in two iconic collaborations with director Alfred Hitchcock, *The Birds* (1963) and *Marnie* (1964). In addition to substantial subsequent work in film and TV, Hedren has also dedicated herself to animal welfare activism. She is the mother of actress Melanie Griffith and grandmother of actress Dakota Johnson.

AUDREY HEPBURN was a film and fashion icon whose astounding appearances on screen include the classics *Roman Holiday* (1953), for which she won an Oscar; *Breakfast at Tiffany's* (1961); and *My Fair Lady* (1964). She won a Tony Award in 1954 for the Broadway play *Ondine*. Her movie-stardom slowed after the 1960s, when she devoted much of her time to UNICEF as a Goodwill Ambassador, for which she received the US Presidential Medal of Freedom.

KATHARINE HEPBURN soared as strong, sophisticated, and spirited characters in a celebrated career that spanned over sixty years. She received twelve Academy Award nominations and won four times, for *Morning Glory* (1933), *Guess Who's Coming to Dinner* (1967), *The Lion in Winter* (1968), and *On Golden Pond* (1981).

LENA HORNE was an actress, vocalist, and activist whose career stretched over seven decades. She appeared in films including *Cabin in the Sky* (1943), *Stormy Weather* (1943), and *The Wiz* (1978). Off screen, she won a Special Tony Award for Distinguished Achievement in Theatre, earned two Grammys, and was active in the civil rights movement.

KATY JURADO was a boundary-breaking Mexican actress active in Mexican cinema in the 1940s and '50s and in Hollywood Westerns in the 1950s and '60s. For 1952's *High Noon*, she became the first Latin American actress to win a Golden Globe, and for 1954's *Broken Lance*, she was the first to be nominated for an Oscar.

GRACE KELLY made her mark on movies in the 1950s. She was nominated for an Academy Award for *Mogambo* (1953) and won for *The Country Girl* (1954). She starred in three of Alfred Hitchcock's iconic thrillers, *Rear Window* (1954), *Dial M for Murder* (1954), and *To Catch a Thief* (1955). In 1956, she married Prince Rainier III, became Princess of Monaco, and turned her focus to charity work in service of children and the arts.

NANCY KWAN is a Chinese American actress who skyrocketed to stardom in *The World of Suzie Wong* (1960), for which she was nominated for a Golden Globe, and *Flower Drum Song* (1961). Kwan's performances in these simultaneously pioneering and racially problematic films marked monumental moments of representation for Asian actors in Hollywood.

VIVIEN LEIGH, though British, won two Oscars for performances as Southern belles: Scarlett in *Gone with the Wind* (1939) and Blanche in *A Streetcar Named Desire* (1951). Also successful on stage, she often performed opposite her second husband, Laurence Olivier, and won a Tony for *Tovarich* (1963).

CAROLE LOMBARD sizzled in screwball comedies of the 1930s and '40s, including *Twentieth Century* (1934) and *My Man Godfrey* (1936), for which she was nominated for an Academy Award. Her final film, *To Be or Not to Be* (1942), was released a month after her death at thirty-three in an airplane accident.

ANITA LOOS was an actress, screenwriter, playwright, and novelist who became Hollywood's first female staff screenwriter in 1912 and contributed to over one hundred films. In her varied career, she wrote the 1925 novel *Gentlemen Prefer Blondes*, the screenplay for 1939's *The Women* (with Jane Murfin), and the 1951 theatrical adaptation of *Gigi*, which starred Audrey Hepburn in her Broadway debut.

SOPHIA LOREN is an Italian actress who was the first actor to win an Oscar for a performance in a non-English language, for her work in 1960's *Two Women*. She was nominated for a second Oscar for *Marriage Italian Style* (1964) and received an Academy Honorary Award as "one of the genuine treasures of world cinema" in 1991.

HATTIE McDANIEL overcame racism on screen and off to become the first African American to win an Academy Award, for her role as Mammy in 1939's *Gone with the Wind*. The staggeringly successful film whitewashed slavery and the Civil War–era South, and while some praised McDaniel's performance and Oscar win as vital moments of visibility, others objected to the pernicious stereotypes the film perpetuated. She was barred from the film's premiere by Atlanta's Jim Crow laws and sidelined to a segregated table at the Oscars. Her work also includes *Show Boat* (1936) and *The Great Lie* (1941).

BARBARA "BOBBIE" McLEAN was a film editor known in the industry as "Hollywood's editor-in-chief." Over the course of her career from the 1930s through the '50s, she edited over sixty films, won an Oscar for 1944's *Wilson*, and received an additional six Academy Award nominations, including for *All About Eve* (1950).

CARMEN MIRANDA was a Portuguese-born Brazilian singer, dancer, and actor. She starred in fourteen American films in the 1940s and '50s, in which she sang her signature sambas in her famously fruit-festooned hats. In 1941, she became the first Latin American star to leave her handprints in the cement of the Hollywood Walk of Fame at Grauman's Chinese Theatre in Los Angeles.

MARILYN MONROE, one of classic Hollywood's most enduring and elegant icons, appeared in over two dozen films in her short but significant career, including *Gentlemen Prefer Blondes* (1953), *The Seven Year Itch* (1955), and *Some Like It Hot* (1959). While celebrated for her comedic chops, Monroe also won acclaim in an atypically dramatic performance in *Bus Stop* (1956).

RITA MORENO appeared in movie musicals including *Singin' in the Rain* (1952) and *The King and I* (1956) before delivering an Academy Award–winning performance as Anita in 1961's *West Side Story*. In 1977, she became the third person, second performer, and first Latin American to "EGOT," or have won an Emmy, Grammy, Oscar, and Tony.

KIM NOVAK starred in 1950s films including *Picnic* (1955), *The Man with the Golden Arm* (1955), and *Pal Joey* (1957) before delivering one of Hollywood's most haunting performances as Madeleine/Judy in the Alfred Hitchcock thriller *Vertigo* (1958).

MARY PICKFORD was an actress and producer. She co-founded Pickford-Fairbanks Studios in 1919 and was one of thirty-six founders of the Academy of Motion Picture Arts and Sciences in 1927. She won the Oscar for Best Actress for 1929's *Coquette* and, in 1976, received an Academy Honorary Award "in recognition of her unique contributions to the film industry."

DONNA REED is best remembered for her performance as Mary Hatch in the festive favorite *It's a Wonderful Life* (1946). She won an Oscar for 1953's *From Here to Eternity* and was a four-time Emmy nominee for *The Donna Reed Show*.

DEBBIE REYNOLDS was an actress and entrepreneur whose career spanned seven decades. She starred as Kathy in 1952's *Singin' in the Rain,* was nominated for an Academy Award for 1964's *The Unsinkable Molly Brown,* and received the Academy's Jean Hersholt Humanitarian Award in 2015. Her daughter was actress Carrie Fisher, and her granddaughter is actress Billie Lourd.

GINGER ROGERS danced opposite Fred Astaire in hit movie musicals of the 1930s and '40s, including *Top Hat* (1935), *Shall We Dance* (1937), and *The Barkleys of Broadway* (1949). She also won acclaim in nonmusical films, including *Kitty Foyle* (1940), for which she earned an Oscar.

ROSALIND RUSSELL played legendary ladies on stage and screen in an acting career that lasted over forty years. She starred in the title role in *Auntie Mame* on Broadway in 1956, then on film in 1958; was nominated for four Academy Awards; and won a Tony Award for her performance in 1953's *Wonderful Town*. In 1973, she received the Academy's Jean Hersholt Humanitarian Award.

EVA MARIE SAINT won an Oscar for her film debut in *On the Waterfront* (1954). Her career in film, television, and theater—with highlights including *A Hatful of Rain* (1957), *North by Northwest* (1959), five Emmy nominations, and one win—has spanned over seventy years.

NORMA SHEARER specialized in sophistication and sass in starring roles in the 1920s, '30s, and '40s, in films including *Romeo and Juliet* (1936), *Marie Antoinette* (1938), and *The Women* (1939). She was a six-time Academy Award nominee, and in 1930 she was nominated for Best Actress for two films, winning for *The Divorcee*.

BARBARA STANWYCK was a four-time Oscar nominee, an Academy Honorary Award recipient for her "unique contribution to the art of screen acting," and a three-time Emmy winner. Revered for her versatility, she starred in memorable movies including *Stella Dallas* (1937), *Ball of Fire* (1941), *The Lady Eve* (1941), and *Double Indemnity* (1944).

GLORIA SWANSON was a star in the 1910s and '20s as Hollywood transitioned from silent to sound films. She was nominated for three Academy Awards: for 1928's *Sadie Thompson,* which she also produced; for 1929's *The Trespasser,* her first "talkie"; and for her comeback role as the notorious Norma Desmond in 1950's *Sunset Boulevard.*

ELIZABETH TAYLOR launched her career as a child actress in the 1940s and became one of Hollywood's biggest stars in the '50s and '60s, in films including *Cat on a Hot Tin Roof* (1958) and *Who's Afraid of Virginia Woolf?* (1966). She was a five-time Oscar nominee and two-time winner, and she became one of the first celebrity HIV/AIDS activists, for which she received the Academy's Jean Hersholt Humanitarian Award in 1993.

SHIRLEY TEMPLE was one of the 1930s' youngest and most popular stars and received the first Academy Juvenile Award in 1935. Her many films as a child star included *Bright Eyes* (1934), *Curly Top* (1935), and *Heidi* (1937). After she retired from moviemaking, she turned to diplomacy, including serving as a United States ambassador.

MIYOSHI UMEKI was the first Asian American woman to win an Oscar for performance, for her role in 1957's *Sayonara.* The actress and singer also starred as Mei-Li in *Flower Drum Song* on stage in 1958, which earned her a Tony nomination, and on screen in 1961, which earned her a Golden Globe nod.

LUPE VÉLEZ—a Mexican actress, singer, and dancer—made her mark on movies of the 1920s, '30s, and '40s as one of Hollywood's first Latin American stars. After moving from silent to sound films, she starred as Carmelita in eight Mexican Spitfire films from 1939 to 1943.

ETHEL WATERS was a singer and actress who broke down racial barriers on Broadway, in film, and on TV. She was the second African American to be nominated for an Oscar—for 1949's *Pinky*—and the first to be nominated for an Emmy.

ONNA WHITE was a choreographer who received an Academy Honorary Award for her work on 1968's *Oliver!* in a rare instance of the Academy's recognizing choreography. She also created dances for *The Music Man* on stage and screen and was nominated for eight Tonys for her work on Broadway.

ESTHER WILLIAMS, nicknamed the "Million Dollar Mermaid," was a competitive swimmer-turned-actress best known for starring in singing, dancing, swimming "aquamusicals" for MGM—including *Million Dollar Mermaid* (1952)—in the 1940s and '50s.

ANNA MAY WONG is considered the first Hollywood—and international—Chinese American film star. Though she was often relegated to stereotypical supporting roles, she starred in 1937's *Daughter of Shanghai,* which was unusual for its time in featuring Asian actors as leads.

NATALIE WOOD starred in iconic films of the 1940s, '50s, and '60s, including 1947's *Miracle on 34th Street* as a child, 1955's *Rebel without a Cause* as a teen (for which she received one of her three Oscar nominations), and 1961's *West Side Story* as an adult.

LORETTA YOUNG had a vast, varied career from the 1910s through the '80s in film and on TV. She won an Academy Award for *The Farmer's Daughter* (1947), was nominated for *Come to the Stable* (1949), and earned three Emmys for TV's *The Loretta Young Show.*

For Jason, who turned my world from
sepia-tone to Technicolor —J.R.A.

For my husband, Jared, who has given me not
only the stars, but the moon as well —P.E.

Text copyright © 2023 by John Robert Allman
Jacket art and interior illustrations copyright © 2023 by Peter Emmerich

All rights reserved. Published in the United States by Doubleday, an imprint of Random House
Children's Books, a division of Penguin Random House LLC, New York.

DOUBLEDAY YR with colophon is a registered trademark of Penguin Random House LLC.

Visit us on the Web! rhcbooks.com

Educators and librarians, for a variety of teaching tools, visit us at RHTeachersLibrarians.com

Library of Congress Cataloging-in-Publication Data
Names: Allman, John Robert, author. | Emmerich, Peter, illustrator.
Title: J is for Judy : classic Hollywood's leading ladies from A to Z /
written by John Robert Allman ; illustrated by Peter Emmerich.
Description: First edition. | New York : Doubleday Books for Young Readers, [2023]
Audience: Ages 4–8. | Summary: "An alphabetic celebration of Hollywood's leading actresses
of the classic silver screen era, from Audrey Hepburn to Zsa Zsa Gabor" —Provided by publisher.
Identifiers: LCCN 2022033950 (print) | LCCN 2022033951 (ebook) |
ISBN 978-0-593-56518-6 (hardcover) | ISBN 978-0-593-56519-3 (library binding) |
ISBN 978-0-593-56520-9 (ebook)
Subjects: LCSH: Motion picture actors and actresses—United States—Biography—Juvenile literature. |
Actresses—United States—Biography—Juvenile literature. | Alphabet books. | LCGFT: Alphabet books.
Classification: LCC PN1998.2 .A4356 2023 (print) | LCC PN1998.2 (ebook) |
DDC 791.4302/8092273 [B]—dc23/eng/20220809

MANUFACTURED IN CHINA
10 9 8 7 6 5 4 3 2 1
First Edition